Instant Audio Processing with Web Audio

Learn how to use the Web Audio API to implement audio effects such as loop stitching, audio ducking, and audio equalization through practical, hands-on recipes

Chris Khoo

PUBLISHING

BIRMINGHAM - MUMBAI

Instant Audio Processing with Web Audio

First published: August 2013

Production Reference: 1220813

Published by Packt Publishing Ltd.
Livery Place
35 Livery Street
Birmingham B3 2PB, UK.

ISBN 978-1-78216-879-9

www.packtpub.com

Credits

Author
Chris Khoo

Reviewer
Alex Libby

Acquisition Editor
James Jones

Commissioning Editor
Harsha Bharwani

Technical Editor
Veena Pagare

Project Coordinator
Suraj Bisht

Proofreader
Joanna McMahon

Graphics
Abhinash Sahu

Production Coordinator
Nitesh Thakur

Cover Work
Nitesh Thakur

Cover Image
Sheetal Aute

About the Author

Chris Khoo has been an avid programmer since his first encounter with the personal computer in the 80s. Since then, he's evolved from a nerdy hobbyist programmer into a full-fledged software developer with over 15 years of industry experience in developing games at companies including Microsoft, Disney, Electronic Arts, and Nexon. To date, he has shipped over a dozen console, mobile, and online games including the FIFA series, the SSX series, Def Jam: FFNY, Tom and Jerry Online, and Hyper Grav. His unique combination of AAA console game programming experience and web development experience makes him uniquely qualified to pen a practical study of implementing audio using the Web Audio API.

Chris presently resides in Vancouver, BC, with his wife and two children. He is the founder and primary developer at Wappworks Studio, a 3-man indie game studio dedicated to online and mobile web games. When he's not busy at work, Chris enjoys playing board games and helping out with praise and worship at his local church.

I would like to send a giant heartfelt thanks to my wife, Joanne, and my two kids, Michelle and Michael, for allowing me to give up my family time in pursuit of an authoring career. I would also like to thank my business partner and confidante, Chris, for his patience and advice. Finally, I want to thank God for all His blessings and for giving me peace and comfort as I've frantically juggled my personal, work, and authoring roles.

About the Reviewer

Alex Libby's background is in IT support—he has been involved in supporting end users for the last 15 years in a variety of different environments, and currently works as a Technical Analyst, supporting a medium-sized SharePoint estate for an international distributor based in the UK. Although Alex gets to play with different technologies in his day job, his true love has always been the Open Source movement, and in particular, experimenting with jQuery, CSS3, and HTML5. To date, Alex has written several books for Packt, including ones on HTML5 technologies and others on jQuery tools. In his free time, Alex enjoys helping out at the local amateur theatre. He also enjoys cycling and photography.

www.PacktPub.com

Support files, eBooks, discount offers and more

You might want to visit www.PacktPub.com for support files and downloads related to your book.

Did you know that Packt offers eBook versions of every book published, with PDF and ePub files available? You can upgrade to the eBook version at www.PacktPub.com and as a print book customer, you are entitled to a discount on the eBook copy. Get in touch with us at service@packtpub.com for more details.

At www.PacktPub.com, you can also read a collection of free technical articles, sign up for a range of free newsletters and receive exclusive discounts and offers on Packt books and eBooks.

http://PacktLib.PacktPub.com

Do you need instant solutions to your IT questions? PacktLib is Packt's online digital book library. Here, you can access, read and search across Packt's entire library of books.

Why Subscribe?

- ▸ Fully searchable across every book published by Packt
- ▸ Copy and paste, print and bookmark content
- ▸ On demand and accessible via web browser

Free Access for Packt account holders

If you have an account with Packt at www.PacktPub.com, you can use this to access PacktLib today and view nine entirely free books. Simply use your login credentials for immediate access.

Table of Contents

Preface

Web Audio is a new audio API proposed by **World Wide Web Consortium** (**W3C**) to address the shortcomings of the existing HTML5 Audio API. This new API allows developers to perform advanced real-time audio processing/mixing that is just not possible with current standards.

In this book, we'll explore Web Audio's audio processing functionality through a series of recipes. We'll also apply our learning towards building an audio system. By the end of the book, we will have a clear grasp of the Web Audio API, its design philosophy, and how to utilize it to put together a plethora of audio effects.

Web Audio is a fairly new API. As a result, many browsers do not yet support it. The list of web browsers which currently support it is a short one; they are Chrome for PC and Mac (v10 or higher), and Safari for PC and Mac (v6 or higher).Firefox has slated to support Web Audio in its next release (Version 19).

The Web Audio API is a big subject matter for an Instant book. In fact, it's so large that we'll jump straight into Web Audio's audio manipulation functionality. But don't worry, we're providing *bonus online recipes* which focus on the basic aspects of the API which we skipped over.

What this book covers

Setting Up a Web Host (Simple), will help us set up a local web host for our development environment.

Playing Audio in a Loop (Simple), will help us explore Web Audio's audio looping functionality as we build a simple sound player.

Setting the Volume (Simple), will guide us through an in-depth look at Web Audio's volume control functionality.

Automating Audio Parameters (Intermediate), will focus on Web Audio's timing and scheduling functionality, and use it to build a sound ducking audio processor.

Building an Equalizer Using BiquadFilterNode (Advanced), will cover Web Audio's built-in audio processing functionality while building a 5-band equalizer.

In addition, this book features the following bonus online recipes. These recipes are available at http://www.packtpub.com/sites/default/files/downloads/ Bonus_Recipes.pdf.

Initializing Web Audio (Simple), will take a look at Web Audio initialization on various web browsers.

Playing Audio Files (Simple), will cover Web Audio's design and playback fundamentals as we implement a sound player.

Scheduling Audio Playback (Intermediate), will explore Web Audio's timing functionality as we build a sound player capable of stitching audio playback seamlessly.

What you need for this book

The following applications are required in order to follow all the recipes:

▸ Chrome or Safari web browser (we need a Web Audio-capable web browser in order to run the recipes).

▸ Apache Web Server (we have to host the recipes on a local web server in order to function properly. Most of the recipes rely on audio data loaded via AJAX and AJAX functions properly, only if the requested data is hosted on a web server. I've chosen to use Apache as the local web server of choice, as it is available for virtually all operating systems).

If you are installing it for the first time, I recommend installing **XAMPP**. XAMPP is a free and open source web server package which includes Apache Web Server as part of its bundle. The XAMPP installer and set up instructions are available at http://www.apachefriends.org/en/xampp.html.

You'll also need a text editor as we'll be writing CSS, HTML, and JavaScript code. While simple text editors such as Notepad or Vim will suffice, I recommend choosing a JavaScript editor with good autocomplete functionality, as we'll be spending a large part of our time writing JavaScript. A good and free JavaScript editor is Komo Edit (http://www.activestate.com/komodo-edit).

Who this book is for

This book is meant for programmers who already have some HTML and JavaScript programming experience and who are seeking to learn how to use Web Audio in their applications. Experience with AJAX and web server installation/configuration will be good, but is not a necessity in order to follow the contents.

Conventions

In this book, you will find a number of styles of text that distinguish between different kinds of information. Here are some examples of these styles, and an explanation of their meaning.

Code words in text are shown as follows: " The recipes of this book assume that the recipe application root is the webaudio subdirectory."

A block of code is set as follows:

```
Alias /mywebaudio /webaudio

<Directory "/webaudio">
    Order allow,deny
    Allow from all
</Directory>
```

When we wish to draw your attention to a particular part of a code block, the relevant lines or items are set in bold:

```
sourceNode.loop = true;
// Specify a custom loop segment
sourceNode.loopStart = audioBuffer.duration * 0.5;
sourceNode.loopEnd = audioBuffer.duration;
// Keep track of the active sound loop
```

New terms and **important words** are shown in bold. Words that you see on the screen, in menus or dialog boxes for example, appear in the text like this: "clicking the **Next** button moves you to the next screen".

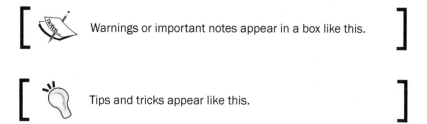

Warnings or important notes appear in a box like this.

Tips and tricks appear like this.

Reader feedback

Feedback from our readers is always welcome. Let us know what you think about this book—what you liked or may have disliked. Reader feedback is important for us to develop titles that you really get the most out of.

To send us general feedback, simply send an e-mail to `feedback@packtpub.com`, and mention the book title via the subject of your message.

If there is a topic that you have expertise in and you are interested in either writing or contributing to a book, see our author guide on `www.packtpub.com/authors`.

Customer support

Now that you are the proud owner of a Packt book, we have a number of things to help you to get the most from your purchase.

Downloading the example code

You can download the example code files for all Packt books you have purchased from your account at `http://www.packtpub.com`. If you purchased this book elsewhere, you can visit `http://www.packtpub.com/support` and register to have the files e-mailed directly to you.

Errata

Although we have taken every care to ensure the accuracy of our content, mistakes do happen. If you find a mistake in one of our books—maybe a mistake in the text or the code—we would be grateful if you would report this to us. By doing so, you can save other readers from frustration and help us improve subsequent versions of this book. If you find any errata, please report them by visiting `http://www.packtpub.com/submit-errata`, selecting your book, clicking on the **errata submission form** link, and entering the details of your errata. Once your errata are verified, your submission will be accepted and the errata will be uploaded on our website, or added to any list of existing errata, under the Errata section of that title. Any existing errata can be viewed by selecting your title from `http://www.packtpub.com/support`.

Piracy

Piracy of copyright material on the Internet is an ongoing problem across all media. At Packt, we take the protection of our copyright and licenses very seriously. If you come across any illegal copies of our works, in any form, on the Internet, please provide us with the location address or website name immediately so that we can pursue a remedy.

Please contact us at `copyright@packtpub.com` with a link to the suspected pirated material.

We appreciate your help in protecting our authors, and our ability to bring you valuable content.

Questions

You can contact us at `questions@packtpub.com` if you are having a problem with any aspect of the book, and we will do our best to address it.

Instant Audio Processing with Web Audio

Welcome to *Instant Audio Processing with Web Audio*. In this book, we'll explore Web Audio's capabilities through a series of step-by-step recipes. As we progress through the recipes, we'll construct a reusable audio layer which can be reused in other Web Audio applications.

Setting up a web host (Simple)

We'll need to set up a web server to host our Web Audio recipes, because we will be exploring Web Audio's audio file manipulation capabilities. Loading of the audio files rely on AJAX and AJAX-only functions reliably when the said audio files are served by a web host. Ergo, we'll need a web host for the recipes.

If we don't yet have a web server set up, this recipe will help us do just that.

We'll set up an Apache Server to host our recipes at `http://localhost/mywebaudio`, which will be the **recipe application URL**. As we don't have a Web Audio recipe yet, we'll set it up to host our **recipe base framework** instead. The recipe base framework implements all the necessary plumbing so that we can focus on using Web Audio. I've included an overview of the framework at the end of this recipe.

 Already have a web server set up? Go ahead and create a new subdirectory for the recipes and host it at `http://localhost/mywebaudio`.

Getting ready

If you don't yet have Apache Web Server installed on your machine, now is the time to do that. The easiest way to install it is through installers such as XAMPP (http://www.apachefriends.org).

In addition, please create a subdirectory to act as the **recipe application root** for the recipes in this book. The recipes in this book assume that the recipe application root is the webaudio subdirectory that is placed just off the root of the drive. However, feel free to select a different path for the recipe application root.

The configuration changes that we'll be applying to Apache are available in tools/ApacheConfiguration/apache.conf.

How to do it...

1. Copy the recipe framework from tools/RecipeFramework to the recipe application root.

2. Navigate to the web server's conf directory, and add the following to http.conf— the snippet links of the recipe application root to the recipe application URL:

    ```
    Alias /mywebaudio /webaudio

    <Directory "/webaudio">
        Order allow,deny
        Allow from all
    </Directory>
    ```

3. Replace all the snippet references to /webaudio with the absolute path to the recipe application root.

4. Restart Apache Web Server.

Downloading the example code

You can download the example code files for all Packt books you have purchased from your account at http://www.packtpub.com. If you purchased this book elsewhere, you can visit http://www. packtpub. com/support and register to have the files e-mailed directly to you.

Open the recipe application URL (`http://localhost/mywebaudio`) in a web browser. You should see the following output on the browser screen:

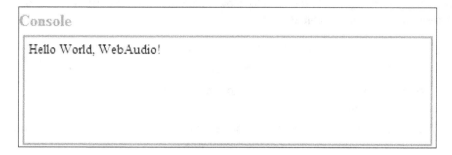

How it works...

The configuration snippet maps the recipe application root to `mywebaudio`—a virtual directory on the web server:

```
Alias /mywebaudio /webaudio
```

We set up the access permissions of the directory so that it's publicly available as shown in the following code. Note that the directory access permissions are always linked to the physical directory path:

```
<Directory "/webaudio">
   Options Indexes
   Order allow,deny
   Allow from all
</Directory>
```

Now that we have our web hosting set up, we can start writing recipes.

There's more...

A copy of the base framework template is stored at `tools/RecipeFramework` in the code bundle.

The recipe base framework

The recipes in this book are built on top of a base framework. This framework provides the application plumbing that is required to allow us to focus on exploring Web Audio. The framework's core functionalities are:

- jQuery for handling all the DOM manipulations
- jQuery UI for building the user interface of the recipes
- The `consoleout()` helper function to output messages to the output window of the framework
- The `assert()` helper function to test for runtime conditions and to report the failures to the output window of the framework
- The `later()` helper function for deferring function execution outside of the calling execution scope

The following table summarizes the base file organization of the framework:

Directory/File	Description
`assets`	This directory contains all the audio assets which we may be used in the recipes.
`thirdparty/jquery-1.9.1.min.js`	This contains the jQuery open source library (MIT license).
`thirdparty/jquery-ui-1.10.2.custom.min.js` `thirdparty/css/pepper-grinder`	This contains the jQuery UI open source library with the *pepper grinder* theme (MIT license).
`app.css`	This file contains all the CSS styles utilized by the recipes.
`utils.js`	This file contains the `consoleout()`, `assert()`, and `later()` helper functions.
`index.html`	This file is the framework launch page. Recipe implementations are added to this file.

The base framework splits the application implementation into two sections. These two sections are found in `index.html`:

- The **JavaScript section** contains the JavaScript implementation of the application. The section is the `<script>` element in the header of the page containing the `WebAudioApp` class implementation.
- The **HTML section** contains the application's HTML implementation. This section is the `appwindow <div>` element in the body of the page.

Playing audio in a loop (Simple)

Now that we can play sounds using an audio buffer, let's take a look at playing them in a loop. In this recipe, we'll create an application with a toggle button which toggles the playback of a choir loop.

Getting ready

The complete source code for this recipe is available in the code bundle at `recipes/Recipe3_1`.

How to do it...

1. Start with a clean copy of the base framework template. The template bundle is located at `tools/RecipeFramework` in the code bundle.

2. Open `index.html` with a text editor.

3. In the HTML section, declare the HTML toggle control:

```
<div id="appwindow">
    <h2>Playing Audio In A Loop</h2>
    <form>
        <input type="checkbox" id="choir" />
        <label for="choir">Choir Loop</label>
    </form>
</div>
```

4. We'll need the Web Audio initialization and the audio file loading routines covered in previous recipes—we'll add these to the JavaScript section:

```
function loadAudioFromUrl( url, loadedCallbackFn,
                           callbackContext ) {
    var request = new XMLHttpRequest();
    request.open("GET", url, true);
    request.responseType = "arraybuffer";

    request.onload = function() {
        consoleout( "Loaded audio '" + url + "'" );
        later( 0, loadedCallbackFn, callbackContext,
                request.response );
    };

    request.onerror = function() {
        consoleout( "ERROR: Failed to load audio from "
```

```
                                   + url );
        };

        request.send();
    }

    WebAudioApp.prototype.initWebAudio = function() {
        var audioContextClass = window.webkitAudioContext
                                  || window.AudioContext;

        if( audioContextClass == null )
            return false;

        this.audioContext = new audioContextClass();
        return true;
    };
```

5. We'll implement the HTML toggle control initialization and loop playback logic in WebAudioApp.initBufferedAudioLoopToggle():

```
WebAudioApp.prototype.initBufferedAudioLoopToggle =
function( elemId, audioSrc ) {
    // Initialize the button and disable it by default
    var jqButton = $( elemId ).button({ disabled: true });

    // Load the audio
    var audioBuffer;
    loadAudioFromUrl( audioSrc, function(audioData){
        // Decode the audio data into an audio buffer
        this.audioContext.decodeAudioData(
                audioData,
                function( audioBufferIn ) {
                    consoleout( "Decoded audio for '"
                                + audioSrc + "'" );

                    // Cache the audio buffer
                    audioBuffer = audioBufferIn;

                    // Audio ready? Enable the button
                    jqButton.button(
                            "option",
                            "disabled",
                            false );
                }
        );
```

```
        }, this );

        // Register a click event listener to trigger playback
        var me = this;
        var activeNode;
        jqButton.click(function( event ) {

            // Stop the active source node...
            if( activeNode != null ) {
                if( activeNode.stop instanceof Function )
                    activeNode.stop( 0 );
                if( activeNode.noteOff instanceof Function )
                    activeNode.noteOff( 0 );

                activeNode = null;

                consoleout( "Stopped audio loop '"
                        + audioSrc + "'" );
            }

            // Start new playback if the button is checked
            if($(this).is(':checked')) {
                var sourceNode = me.audioContext
                                    .createBufferSource();
                sourceNode.buffer = audioBuffer;

                // Connect it to the speakers
                sourceNode.connect( me.audioContext.destination );

                // Start the audio playback
                if( sourceNode.start instanceof Function )
                    sourceNode.start( 0 );
                if( sourceNode.noteOn instanceof Function )
                    sourceNode.noteOn( 0 );

                // Turn on looping
                sourceNode.loop = true;

                // Keep track of the active sound loop
                activeNode = sourceNode;

                consoleout( "Played audio loop '"
                        + audioSrc + "'" );
            }
        });
    };
```

6. Finally, we'll initialize Web Audio to set up the loop playback logic in
   `WebAudioApp.start()`:

```
WebAudioApp.prototype.start = function() {
    if( !this.initWebAudio() ) {
        consoleout( "Browser does not support WebAudio" );
        return;
    }

    this. initBufferedAudioLoopToggle( "#choir", "assets/
looperman-morpheusd-amazing-pt2-choir-120-bpm.wav" );
    };
```

Launch the application test URL in a web browser (`http://localhost/myaudiomixer`)
and click on the **Choir Loop** button to toggle the loop playback. The following is a screenshot
of what we should see in the web browser:

Playing Audio In A Loop

    Choir Loop

Console

Played audio loop 'assets/looperman-morpheusd-amazing-pt2-choir-120-bpm.wav'
Decoded audio for 'assets/looperman-morpheusd-amazing-pt2-choir-120-bpm.wav'
Loaded audio 'assets/looperman-morpheusd-amazing-pt2-choir-120-bpm.wav'

How it works...

Let's take a closer look at the toggle control's `click` event handler in `WebAudioApp.`
`initBufferedAudioLoopToggle()`:

1. When the user deactivates playback, we use the method `stop()` or
   `noteOff()` of the `AudioBufferSourceNode` instance to explicitly
   stop the active `AudioNode` class:

```
jqButton.click(function( event ) {

    // Stop the active source node.
    if( activeNode != null ) {
        if( activeNode.stop instanceof Function )
            activeNode.stop( 0 );
```

```
        if ( activeNode.noteOff instanceof Function )
            activeNode.noteOff( 0 );

        activeNode = null;

        . . .
    }
```

2. When a user activates playback, we trigger sound playback as per the previous recipe:

```
if ($(this).is(':checked')) {
    // Decode the audio data into an audio buffer
    var sourceNode = me.audioContext.createBufferSource();
    sourceNode.buffer = audioBuffer;

    // Connect it to the AudioContext destination node
    sourceNode.connect( me.audioContext.destination );

    // Start the audio playback
    if ( sourceNode.start instanceof Function )
        sourceNode.start( 0 );
    if ( sourceNode.noteOn instanceof Function )
        sourceNode.noteOn( 0 );
```

3. Then, we turn on the looping behavior by setting the `AudioBufferSourceNode` instance's `loop` attribute to `true`:

```
// Turn on looping
sourceNode.loop = true;
```

> Applications may change the `loop` attribute of `AudioBufferSourceNode` to alter its playback behavior at runtime.

The following are the new Web Audio API members covered in this recipe:

1. Set the `loop` attribute of `AudioBufferSourceNode` to `true` to enable looping; by default, the playback will loop from start to end:

```
interface AudioBufferSourceNode : AudioSourceNode {
    var loop:Boolean;
```

2. The `loopStart` and `loopEnd` attributes of `AudioBufferSourceNode` allow the application to customize the audio section to play in a loop. When specified, playback will loop infinitely once inside the loop time frame:

```
var loopStart:Number;
var loopEnd:Number;
};
```

 `loopEnd` must always be at a later time than `loopStart`. Otherwise, the custom loop time frame is ignored.

There's more...

The ability to limit looping to a subsection within a larger playing segment is a powerful mojo—it lets developers implement some pretty complicated playback behavior with just a few lines of code. Let's use this functionality to improve our choir loop quality.

The choir loop audio sample is actually composed of two audio segments of equal lengths:

▶ A lead-in segment with a soft start

▶ A looping segment

As a result, the choir loop is disjointed whenever the sound loops from start to end. Using the `loopStart` and `loopEnd` attributes of `AudioBufferSourceNode`, we can modify the looping behavior so that looping only occurs in the looping segment. The following diagram describes what we're trying to accomplish:

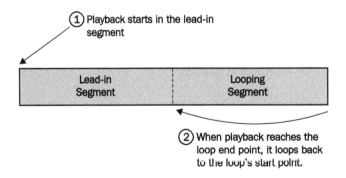

Let's modify the toggle's `click` event handler to fix the loop; add the following highlighted code snippet to the handler:

```
jqButton.click(function( event ) {

    ...

    // Turn on looping
    sourceNode.loop = true;

    // Specify a custom loop segment
    sourceNode.loopStart = audioBuffer.duration * 0.5;
    sourceNode.loopEnd = audioBuffer.duration;

    // Keep track of the active sound loop
    activeNode = sourceNode;

    ...

});
```

We retrieve the sample's duration from the `duration` attribute of `AudioBuffer` and use it to calculate the start and end points for the loop segments. Then, we fill the `loopStart` and `loopEnd` attributes of `AudioBufferSourceNode` with the loop start and end times, respectively.

 The `loopEnd` attribute must be set if the `loopStart` attribute is set. Otherwise, the loop segment settings will have no effect.

Now, the choir loop playback starts with a gentle lead-in before entering a seamless infinite loop.

The AudioBuffer class

The `AudioBuffer` class is much more than a container for audio data. Applications can gather metrics about the audio sample from an `AudioBuffer` instance. Applications can even retrieve and modify the waveform data!

The following is the `AudioBuffer` class definition:

```
interface AudioBuffer {

    var duration:Number;          // readonly
    var numberOfChannels:Number;  // readonly
```

The `duration` attribute contains the audio sample's duration measured in seconds and the `numberOfChannels` attributes contain the number of audio channels in the sample:

```
var sampleRate:Number;          // readonly
var length:Number;              // readonly

function getChannelData(channel:Number):Float32Array;
};
```

The `sampleRate` attribute contains the sample rate of the audio data measured in Hz.

The `length` attribute contains the length of the audio data measured in sample frames.

The function `getChannelData()` retrieves the channel waveform for the target channel. It returns the waveform as an array of the size `length` containing all the frame samples. Each sample is the waveform's PCM float value normalized to the [-1, +1] range.

Setting the volume (Simple)

Now that we've wrapped our heads around playing audio, it's time to look at controlling the sound volume. In this recipe, we'll build an audio player with real-time volume controls. We'll use a piano sound loop instead of the choir loop this time around to keep things fresh.

Getting ready

The complete source code for this recipe is available in the code bundle at `recipes/Recipe4_1a`.

How to do it...

1. Start with a clean copy of the base framework template. The template bundle is located at `tools/RecipeFramework` in the code bundle.

2. Open `index.html` with a text editor.

3. In the HTML section, we'll add the piano loop toggle and the volume control widget:

```
<div id="appwindow">

<h2>Setting The Volume</h2>
<form>
    <input type="checkbox" id="piano" />
```

```
<label for="piano">Piano Loop</label>
<span>VOLUME</span>
<span id="pianovol" style="display: inline-block;
    width: 300px;"></span>
</form>

</div>
```

4. Like the previous recipes, we'll need the Web Audio initialization and audio file loading routines; we'll add these to the JavaScript section:

```
function loadAudioFromUrl( url, loadedCallbackFn,
                              callbackContext ) {
    var request = new XMLHttpRequest();
    request.open("GET", url, true);
    request.responseType = "arraybuffer";

    request.onload = function() {
        consoleout( "Loaded audio '" + url + "'" );
        later( 0, loadedCallbackFn, callbackContext,
            request.response );
    };

    request.onerror = function() {
        consoleout( "ERROR: Failed to load audio from "
                    + url );
    };

    request.send();
}

WebAudioApp.prototype.initWebAudio = function() {
    var audioContextClass = window.webkitAudioContext
                            || window.AudioContext;

    if( audioContextClass == null )
        return false;

    this.audioContext = new audioContextClass();
    return true;
};
```

5. Let's take a first stab at tidying up the boilerplate code for controlling node playback; we'll wrap the `start` and `stop` audio playback functionalities into the functions `stopNode()` and `startNode()`, respectively. It's a marginal improvement, but an improvement nonetheless:

```
function stopNode( node, stopSecs ) {
    if( node.stop instanceof Function )
        node.stop( stopSecs );
    else if( node.noteOff instanceof Function )
        node.noteOff( stopSecs );
}

function startNode( node, startSecs,loop ) {
    // Turn on looping if necessary
    if( loop )
        node.loop = true;

    // Start playback at a predefined time
    if( node.start instanceof Function )
        node.start( startSecs );
    else if( node.noteOn instanceof Function )
        node.noteOn( startSecs );

    return node;
}
```

6. We'll create the function `WebAudioApp.initMusicControls()` to wrap all the sound manipulation logic:

```
WebAudioApp.prototype.initMusicControls =
function( elemId, audioSrc, elemVolId ) {
}
```

7. We'll start by adding the logic for loading the audio data into `WebAudioApp.initMusicControls()` and initializing the sound toggle:

```
// Initialize the button and disable it by default
var jqButton = $( elemId ).button({ disabled: true });

// Load the audio
var audioBuffer;
loadAudioFromUrl( audioSrc, function(audioData){
    // Decode the audio data into an audio buffer
    this.audioContext.decodeAudioData(
        audioData,
```

```
            function( audioBufferIn ) {
                consoleout( "Decoded audio for '"
                            + audioSrc + "'" );

                // Cache the audio buffer
                audioBuffer = audioBufferIn;

                // Enable the button once the audio is ready
                jqButton.button( "option","disabled",false );
            }
        );
    }, this );
```

8. It's time to enhance our node graph with a volume controller. In Web Audio, volume is controlled using a separate `GainNode` node instance. We'll instantiate a `GainNode` instance and attach it to our node graph; the instance will serve as our application's volume controller:

```
// Create the volume control gain node
var context = this.audioContext,
    volNode;

if( context.createGain instanceof Function )
    volNode = context.createGain();
else if( context.createGainNode instanceof Function )
    volNode = context.createGainNode();

// Connect the volume control the the speaker
volNode.connect( context.destination );
```

9. Next, we'll initialize our HTML slider widget and link the slider changes to the `GainNode` instance, of our volume controller:

```
// Create the volume control
$( elemVolId ).slider({
    min: volNode.gain.minValue,
    max: volNode.gain.maxValue,
    step: 0.01,

    value: volNode.gain.value,

    // Add a callback function when the user
    // moves the slider
    slide: function( event, ui ) {
```

```
        // Set the volume directly
        volNode.gain.value = ui.value;

        consoleout( "Adjusted music volume: " + ui.value );
    }
});
```

10. We complete the `WebAudioApp.initMusicControls()` function by implementing the sound toggle event handler for starting and stopping the audio loop:

```
var me = this;
var activeNode;
jqButton.click(function( event ) {

    // Stop the active source node
    if( activeNode != null ) {
        stopNode( activeNode, 0 );
        activeNode = null;

        consoleout( "Stopped music loop '" + audioSrc + "'" );
    }

    // Start a new sound on button activation
    if($(this).is(':checked')) {
        // Start the loop playback
        activeNode = me.audioContext.createBufferSource();
        activeNode.buffer = audioBuffer;
        startNode( activeNode, 0, true );

        // Connect it to the volume control
        activeNode.connect( volNode );

        consoleout( "Played music loop '" + audioSrc + "'" );
    }
});
```

11. Finally, in `WebAudioApp.start()`, we initialize Web Audio and the music controls:

```
WebAudioApp.prototype.start = function() {
    if( !this.initWebAudio() ) {
        consoleout( "Browser does not support WebAudio" );
        return;
    }
```

```
this.initMusicControls(
  "#piano",
  "assets/looperman-morpheusd-dreamworld-fullpiano-120-bpm.wav",
  "#pianovol" );
};
```

Launch the application test URL in a web browser (`http://localhost/myaudiomixer`) to see the end result. The following is a screenshot of what we should see in the browser:

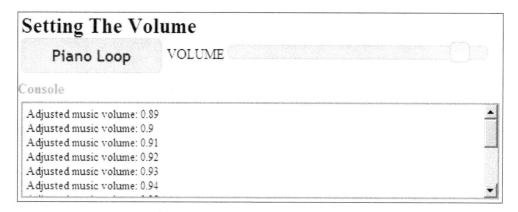

How it works...

We add in volume control support by inserting a `GainNode` instance between the audio source node and the speaker output node, as shown in the following diagram:

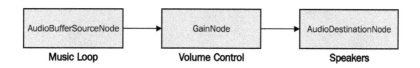

We control the output volume from a `GainNode` instance by adjusting its `gain` audio parameter. The `gain` audio parameter specifies the multiplier applied to the `GainNode` input signal when producing its output signal.

Let's take a deeper look at `WebAudioApp.initLoopToggle()` and its implementation to support volume control:

1. We create `GainNode` using the method `createGain()` or `createGainNode()` of `AudioContext` and cache the instance `volNode`:

    ```
    var context = this.audioContext;
    ```

```
var volNode;
if( context.createGain instanceof Function )
    volNode = context.createGain();
else if( context.createGainNode instanceof Function )
    volNode = context.createGainNode();
```

New `GainNode` instances have their `gain` audio parameter automatically set to 1.

 We check for the `AudioBufferSourceNode` methods `createGainNode()` and `createGain()`. `createGainNode()` is the old name for the method `createGain()`. Again, W3C recommends supporting both function names for backward compatibility.

2. We connect the `GainNode` instance to the context's `AudioDestinationNode` instance:

```
volNode.connect( context.destination );
```

3. Whenever we start playing sounds, we instantiate and activate a new `AudioBufferSourceNode` instance as before, except that we connect its output to the volume controller, `volNode`, instead of directly connecting it to the speaker node. Notice how we're reusing the same `GainNode` instance for all sounds played:

```
var me = this;
var activeNode;
jqButton.click(function( event ) {

    // Stop the active source node
    if( activeNode != null ) {
        me.stopNode( activeNode, 0 );
        activeNode = null;

        . . .
    }

    // Start a new sound on button activation
    if($(this).is(':checked')) {
        // Start the loop playback
        activeNode = me.startNode( audioBuffer, 0, true );

        // Connect it to the volume control
        activeNode.connect( volNode );

        . . .
    }
});
```

The `GainNode` instances are reusable unlike the `AudioBufferSourceNode` instances. The `GainNode` instance will remain alive so long as we maintain an active JavaScript reference through `volNode`.

4. We initialize the volume control element and configure the range and starting values using the `GainNode` instance's `gain` audio parameter settings:

```
$( elemVolId ).slider({
    min: volNode.gain.minValue,
    max: volNode.gain.maxValue,
    step: 0.01,

    value: volNode.gain.value,
```

5. When the slider is moved, we set the `GainNode` instance's `gain.value` attribute to the slider value:

```
slide: function( event, ui ) {

    volNode.gain.value = ui.value;

    . . .

}
});
```

Let's take a look at the Web Audio API methods/attributes introduced in this recipe:

1. `AudioContext.createGain()` instantiates and returns a `GainNode` instance:

```
interface AudioContext {

    function createGain():GainNode;

};
```

2. The `GainNode` instance multiplies its input signal values by a gain multiplier. The `GainNode` instance stores the gain multiplier in an `AudioParam` instance accessible through the `gain` attribute:

```
interface GainNode : AudioNode {

    var gain:AudioParam;

};
```

AudioParam is Web Audio's standard audio parameter interface. It allows applications to retrieve the parameter configuration and to tweak its value. The interface also allows applications to script the parameter behavior.

We'll look at its basic attributes for the moment and explore the scripting functionality in the next recipe:

1. The AudioParam.value attribute stores the applied parameter value of the instance. Applications write to this attribute to change the parameter value directly:

```
interface AudioParam {

    var value:Number;
```

2. The minValue and maxValue attributes store the parameter's minimum and maximum values, respectively.

```
var minValue:Number;        // readonly
    var maxValue:Number;        // readonly
```

 AudioParam does not clamp the value attribute to minValue and maxValue. When an audio parameter is out of range, the resulting behavior is undefined—results are browser specific and may vary depending on the AudioNode class type.

3. The AudioParam instance's default value is stored in defaultValue:

```
var defaultValue:Number;     // readonly
};
```

There's more...

Encapsulating the audio playback logic into the functions startNode() and stopNode() improved the code's readability, but only marginally. In addition, it's tiring having to reimplement the same boilerplate code for initializing Web Audio and for handling audio file loads. It's time to take the next step—we'll integrate the Web Audio boilerplate functionality into the framework template:

1. We'll make the Web Audio initialization and sound loading logic a permanent part of the framework.

2. We'll wrap the node graph construction and sound playback logic into an AudioLayer class.

This is the framework template we'll be using for the rest of the recipes.

The following are the class definitions for the new `AudioLayer` class and the updated `WebAudioApp` class:

▸ The `AudioLayer` constructor constructs the basic Node Graph:

```
class AudioLayer {

    function AudioLayer( context:AudioContext );
```

▸ `AudioLayer` exposes the volume gain audio parameter through its `gain` attribute:

```
    var gain:AudioParam;
```

▸ `AudioLayer.playAudioBuffer()` implements the audio buffer playback logic:

```
    function playAudioBuffer(
            audioBuffer:AudioBuffer,
            startSecs:Number,
            loop:Boolean ):AudioBufferSourceNode
};
```

▸ `WebAudioApp.initWebAudio()` contains the WebAudio initialization logic:

```
class WebAudioApp {

    function start();
    function initWebAudio();
```

▸ `WebAudioApp.loadAudio()` contains the audio buffer loading logic:

```
    function loadAudio(
            audioSrc:String,
            callbackFn:function(buffer:AudioBuffer),
            context:*? );
};
```

We'll also clean up the logic for handling backwards compatibility.

Previously, we searched for the appropriate method name at the time of execution:

```
// Start playback at a predefined time
// Call the appropriate playback start function
// on the AudioBufferSourceNode
if( sourceNode.start instanceof Function )
    sourceNode.start( startSecs );
if( sourceNode.noteOn instanceof Function )
    sourceNode.noteOn( startSecs );
```

This approach is tedious and error prone.

A better approach is to ensure that the new method name always exists. If it does not exist, we'll map the old method to its new name as shown in the following code:

```
// Make sure that an AudioBufferSourceNode instance
// always has the new method name. This code occurs after
// the AudioBufferSourceNode is constructed
if( sourceNode.start == null )
    sourceNode.start = sourceNode.noteOn;

// The rest of the code can now assume that the start()
// function always exists...
```

The updated template framework is found in the `tools/RecipeFrameworkV2` subdirectory in the code bundle.

The directory `recipe/Recipe4_1b` contains this recipe's source code after it's adapted to the new template framework.

Automating the audio parameters (Intermediate)

In previous recipes, we acknowledged that JavaScript timers do not have the fidelity required for scripting audio. Web Audio circumvents this limitation by adding the automation support. Automation allows applications to schedule the predefined audio behaviors ahead of time, thereby allowing applications to schedule audio events independent of the code execution timing.

Most `AudioNode` member attributes are the `AudioParam` instances which support automation. Using this automation support, it's easy to implement sophisticated audio effects such as **ducking**, where the sound level of an audio signal is reduced by the presence of another audio signal. In this recipe, we'll use automation to duck the music whenever the applause sound effect plays.

Getting ready

The complete source code for this recipe is available in the code bundle at `recipes/Recipe5_2`.

How to do it...

1. Start with a clean copy of the base framework template Version 2. The template bundle is located at `tools/RecipeFrameworkV2` in the code bundle.

2. Open `index.html` with a text editor.

3. We'll start by declaring our application controls in the HTML section:

```html
<div id="appwindow">
    <h2>Automating Audio Parameters</h2>
    <form>
        <div>
            <h3>Music</h3>
            <input type="checkbox" id="piano" />
            <label for="piano">Piano Loop</label>
            <span>VOLUME</span>
            <span id="pianovol" style="display: inline-block;
width: 300px;"></span>
        </div>
        <div>
            <h3>Sound Effects</h3>
            <a id="applause" href="javascript:void(0);">Applause</
a>
        </div>
    </form>
</div>
```

4. To implement the ducking support, we'll need to modify the `AudioLayer` class. In the `AudioLayer` constructor, we'll instantiate another `GainNode` instance to act as the ducker volume control:

```javascript
function AudioLayer( audioContext ) {
    this.audioContext = audioContext;

    // Create the ducker GainNode
    this.duckNode = audioContext.createGain();

    // Create the volume GainNode
    this.volNode = audioContext.createGain();

    // Expose the gain control
    this.gain = this.volNode.gain;
```

```
        // Connect the volume control to the ducker
        this.volNode.connect( this.duckNode );

        // Connect the ducker to the speakers
        this.duckNode.connect( this.audioContext.destination );
    }
```

5. We'll add a new function `setDuck()` to `AudioLayer` to activate the ducking behavior:

```
AudioLayer.prototype.setDuck = function( duration ) {
    var TRANSITIONIN_SECS    = 1;
    var TRANSITIONOUT_SECS   = 2;
    var DUCK_VOLUME          = 0.3;

    var duckGain  = this.duckNode.gain;
    var eventSecs = this.audioContext.currentTime;

    // Cancel all future events
    duckGain.cancelScheduledValues( eventSecs );

    // Schedule the volume ramp down
    duckGain.linearRampToValueAtTime(
        DUCK_VOLUME,
        eventSecs + TRANSITIONIN_SECS );

    // Add a set value event to mark ramp up start
    duckGain.setValueAtTime(
        DUCK_VOLUME,
        eventSecs + duration );

    // Schedule the volume ramp up
    duckGain.linearRampToValueAtTime(
        1,
        eventSecs + duration + TRANSITIONOUT_SECS );
};
```

6. Next, we'll add the function `WebAudioApp.initMusic()` for initializing and controlling the music playback:

```
WebAudioApp.prototype.initMusic = function( elemId,
                                            audioSrc,
                                            elemVolId ) {
    // Initialize the button and disable it by default
    var jqButton = $( elemId ).button({ disabled: true });
```

```
// Load the audio
var audioBuffer;
this.loadAudio( audioSrc, function( audioBufferIn ) {
    // Cache the audio buffer
    audioBuffer = audioBufferIn;

    // Enable the button once the audio is ready to go
    jqButton.button( "option", "disabled", false );
}, this );


var musicLayer = this.musicLayer;

// Register a click event listener to trigger playback
var activeNode;
jqButton.click(function( event ) {

    // Stop the active source node
    if( activeNode != null ) {
        activeNode.stop( 0 );
        activeNode = null;

        consoleout( "Stopped music loop '"
                + audioSrc + "'" );
    }

    // Start a new sound on button activation
    if($(this).is(':checked')) {
        // Start the loop playback
        activeNode = musicLayer.playAudioBuffer(
                audioBuffer, 0, true );

        consoleout( "Played music loop '"
                + audioSrc + "'" );
    }
});

// Create the volume control
$( elemVolId ).slider({
    min: musicLayer.gain.minValue,
    max: musicLayer.gain.maxValue,
    step: 0.01,

    value: musicLayer.gain.value,
```

```
                // Add a callback function when the user
                // moves the slider
                slide: function( event, ui ) {
                    // Set the volume directly
                    musicLayer.gain.value = ui.value;

                    consoleout( "Adjusted music volume: "
                                + ui.value );
                }
            });
        };
```

7. We'll add the function `WebAudioApp.initSfx()` for initializing and controlling the sound effects playback. The sound effects controls use the `AudioLayer` ducking functionality to duck the music every time sound effects are active:

```
WebAudioApp.prototype.initSfx = function( elemId,
                                                audioSrc ) {
    // Initialize the button and disable it by default
    var jqButton = $( elemId ).button({ disabled: true });

    // Load the audio
    var audioBuffer;
    this.loadAudio( audioSrc, function( audioBufferIn ) {
        // Cache the audio buffer
        audioBuffer = audioBufferIn;

        // Enable the button once the audio is ready to go
        jqButton.button( "option", "disabled", false );
    }, this );

    // Register a click event listener to trigger playback
    var me = this;
    var activeNode;
    jqButton.click(function( event ) {
        me.sfxLayer.playAudioBuffer( audioBuffer, 0 );

        // Duck the music layer for the duration of the
        // sound effect
        me.musicLayer.setDuck( audioBuffer.duration );

        consoleout( "Ducking music for SFX '"
                    + audioSrc + "'" );
    });
};
```

8. In `WebAudioApp.start()`, we initialize Web Audio, the audio layers, and the application controls:

```
WebAudioApp.prototype.start = function() {
    if( !this.initWebAudio() ) {
        consoleout( "Browser does not support WebAudio" );
        return;
    }

    // Create the audio layers
    this.musicLayer = new AudioLayer( this.audioContext );
    this.sfxLayer = new AudioLayer( this.audioContext );

    // Set up the UI
    this.initMusic( "#piano", "assets/looperman-morpheusd-
dreamworld-fullpiano-120-bpm.wav", "#pianovol" );
        this.initSfx ( "#applause", "assets/applause.mp3" );
    };
```

Launch the application test URL in a web browser (`http://localhost/myaudiomixer`) to see the end result. The following is a screenshot of what we should see in the browser:

How it works...

As previously mentioned, the `AudioParam` interface has automation support which allows applications to build pretty sophisticated automated behaviors. Let's take a look at the `AudioParam` automation methods:

1. The `setValueAtTime()` method sets the audio parameter value to `value` at the time `startTime`:

   ```
   function setValueAtTime( value:Number,
                                     startTime:Number);
   ```

   The following is a diagram illustrating its behavior:

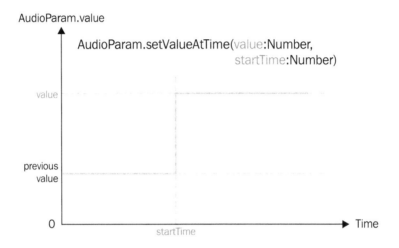

2. The `linearRampToValueAtTime()` method linearly ramps the audio parameter value from the previously set value to the given value, `value`, at the time `endTime`:

   ```
   function linearRampToValueAtTime( value:Number,
                                         endTime:Number);
   ```

The following diagrams illustrate the behavior when ramping up or down to the target value respectively:

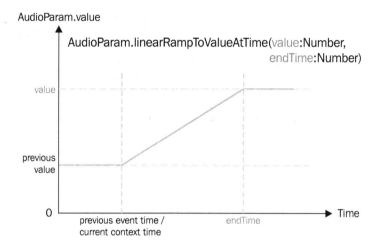

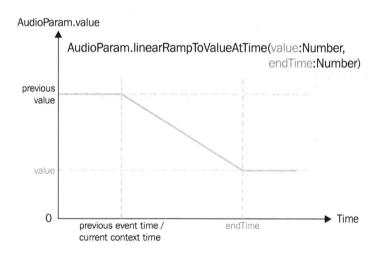

3. The `exponentialRampToValueAtTime()` method exponentially ramps the audio parameter value from the previously set value to the given value, `value`, at the time `endTime`:

```
function exponentialRampToValueAtTime( value:Number,
                                       endTime:Number);
```

The following are the diagrams illustrating its behavior:

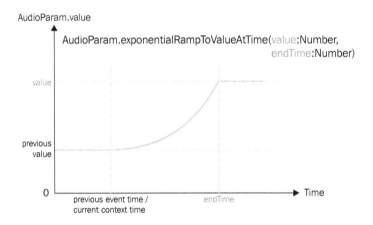

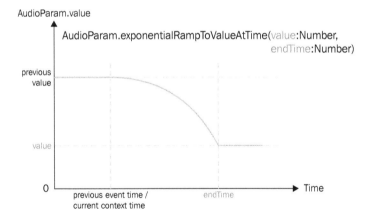

4. The `setTargetAtTime()` method ramps the audio parameter so that it approaches the target value, `value`, starting at the time `startTime`. The `timeConstant` parameter controls the approach rate of the value:

```
function setTargetAtTime( target:Number,
                          startTime:Number,
                          timeConstant:Number);
```

The following are the diagrams illustrating its behavior:

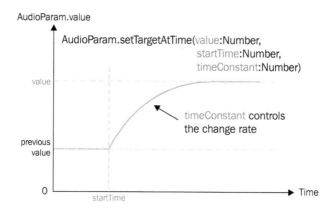

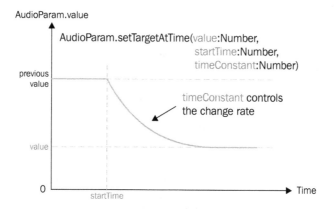

5. The `setValueCurveAtTime()` method applies an array of arbitrary values to the audio parameter. The array values are distributed evenly throughout the automation duration, and the applied value is calculated using linear interpolation:

```
function setValueCurveAtTime( values:Array.<Number>,
                              startTime:Number
                              duration:Number );
```

The following is the diagram illustrating its behavior:

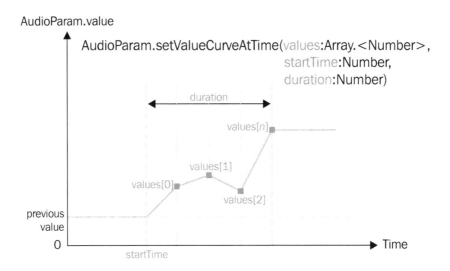

6. The `cancelScheduledValues()` method cancels all the scheduled parameter changes starting at the time `startTime` or later:

```
function cancelScheduledValues( startTime:Number );
```

Like the playback automation methods we discussed in the previous recipe, all time parameters are in seconds and are relative to the audio context's time coordinate system.

Wondering how to specify the start time for some automation methods such as `linearRampToValueAtTime()` and `exponentialRampToValueAtTime()`?

When an automation method does not have a start time parameter, its behavior starts at the nearest previous automation event or the audio context current time, whichever is later.

There are several key rules in regards to scheduling the automation events:

- If an event is added at a time when there is already an event of the exact same type, the new event replaces the old one.

- If an event is added at a time when there is already an event of a different type, it is scheduled to occur immediately after it.

- Events may not overlap – some events occur over time, such as the `linearRampToValueAtTime()` automation behavior. No events may be scheduled in the time when such events are active, otherwise Web Audio will throw a runtime exception.

We leverage the `AudioParam` automation support to implement ducking. The following is the overview of the ducking logic implemented in the `AudioLayer` class:

1. We add a `GainNode` instance into the node graph as the duck controller.
2. When a sound effect is played, we script the duck controller's `gain` audio parameter to reduce the audio output gain level for the duration of the sound effect.
3. If ducking is reactivated while it is still active, we revise the scheduled ducking events so that they end at the appropriate time.

The following is the node graph diagram produced by the code:

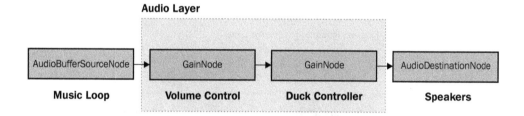

Why use two GainNode instances instead of one?

It's a good idea to split up the independent scripted audio gain behaviors into separate `GainNode` instances. This ensures that the scripted behaviors will interact properly.

Now, let's take a look at `AudioLayer.setDuck()` which implements the ducking behavior:

1. The `AudioLayer.setDuck()` method takes a duration (in seconds) indicating how long the duck behavior should be applied:

```
AudioLayer.prototype.setDuck = function( duration ) {
```

2. We cache the duck controller's `gain` audio parameter in `duckGain`:

```
var TRANSITIONIN_SECS    = 1;
var TRANSITIONOUT_SECS   = 2;
var DUCK_VOLUME          = 0.3;


var duckGain  = this.duckNode.gain;
```

3. We cancel any existing leftover scheduled duck behaviors, thereby allowing us to start with a clean slate:

```
var eventSecs = this.audioContext.currentTime;


duckGain.cancelScheduledValues( eventSecs );
```

4. We employ the `linearRampToValueAtTime()` automation behavior to schedule the transition in—the audio parameter is scripted to linearly ramp from the existing volume to the duck volume, `DUCK_VOLUME`, over the time, `TRANSITIONIN_SECS`. Because there are no future events scheduled, the behavior starts at the current audio context time:

```
duckGain.linearRampToValueAtTime(
    DUCK_VOLUME,
    eventSecs + TRANSITIONIN_SECS );
```

 If the volume is already at `DUCK_VOLUME`, the transition has no effect, thereby creating the effect of *extending* the ducking behavior.

5. We add an automation event to mark the start of the `TRANSITIONOUT` section. We do this by scheduling a `setValueAtTime()` automation behavior:

```
duckGain.setValueAtTime(
    DUCK_VOLUME,
    eventSecs + duration );
```

6. Finally, we set up the TRANSITIONOUT section using a linearRampToValueAtTime() automation behavior. We arrange the transition to occur over TRANSITIONOUT_SECS by scheduling its end time to occur after the TRANSITIONOUT_SECS duration of the previous setValueAtTime() automation behavior:

```
// Schedule the volume ramp up
duckGain.linearRampToValueAtTime(
    1,
    eventSecs + duration + TRANSITIONOUT_SECS );
};
```

The following is a graph illustrating the automation we've applied to duckGain, the duck controller's gain audio parameter:

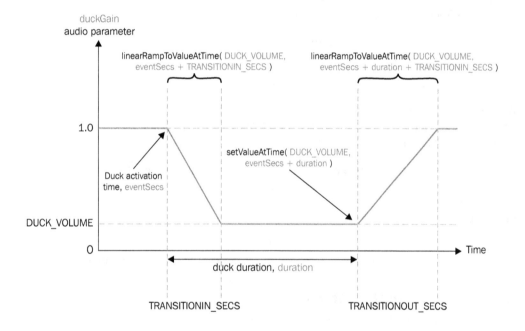

In order to have the sound effects activation duck the music volume, the sound effects and music have to be played on separate audio layers. That's why this recipe instantiates two AudioLayer instances—one for music playback and the other for sound effect playback.

The dedicated music `AudioLayer` instance is cached in the `WebAudioApp` attribute, `musicLayer`, and the dedicated sound effects `AudioLayer` instance is cached in `WebAudioApp` attribute `sfxLayer`:

```
WebAudioApp.prototype.start = function() {
    ...

    this.musicLayer = new AudioLayer( this.audioContext );
    this.sfxLayer = new AudioLayer( this.audioContext );


    ...
};
```

Whenever a sound effects button is clicked, we play the sound and simultaneously activate the duck behavior on the music layer. This logic is implemented as part of the behavior of the sound effect's `click` event handler in `WebAudioApp.initSfx()`:

```
jqButton.click(function( event ) {
    me.sfxLayer.playAudioBuffer( audioBuffer, 0 );

    me.musicLayer.setDuck( audioBuffer.duration );
```

We activate ducking on `webAudioApp.musicLayer`, the music's `AudioLayer` instance. The ducking duration is set to the sound effects duration (we read the sound effects sample duration from its `AudioBuffer` instance).

The ducking behavior is just one demonstration of the power of automation. The possibilities are endless given the breadth of automation-friendly audio parameters available in Web Audio. Other possible effects that are achievable through automation include fades, tempo matching, and cyclic panning effects.

Please refer to the latest online W3C Web Audio documentation at `http://www.w3.org/TR/webaudio/` for a complete list of available audio parameters.

Advanced automation techniques

Web Audio allows the output from an `AudioNode` instance to drive an audio parameter. This is accomplished by connecting an `AudioNode` instance to an `AudioParam` instance:

```
interface AudioNode {
    function connect( destinationNode:AudioParam,
            outputIndex:Number? );
};
```

The previous code connects an `AudioNode` instance to a target `AudioParam` instance. `destinationNode` is the target `AudioParam` instance, and `outputIndex` is the `AudioNode` output to connect to it.

This functionality allows applications to automate audio parameters using controller data from data files—the controller data is loaded into an `AudioBuffer` instance, and is injected into the node graph using an `AudioBufferSourceNode` instance.

The following node graph illustrates this approach for controlling the output volume using controller data from a file:

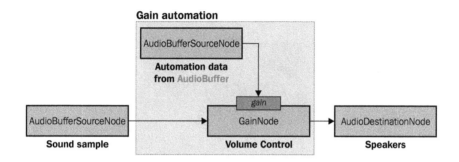

The automation data can be generated even at runtime using JavaScript. The following node graph employs this method to automate a sound sample's output volume:

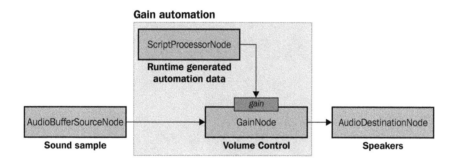

Unfortunately, the implementation details for accomplishing these effects are beyond the scope of this book. Therefore, I leave the task of producing working examples of these cases to you, the readers.

Building an equalizer using BiquadFilterNode (Advanced)

One of the big advantages of using Web Audio is its built-in supporting for constructing sophisticated audio effects in real time. In this recipe, we'll use Web Audio's `BiquadFilterNode` functionality to build a 5-band equalizer. The implementation includes a real-time equalizer frequency response chart display so that we can visualize the equalizer's impact on the sound output.

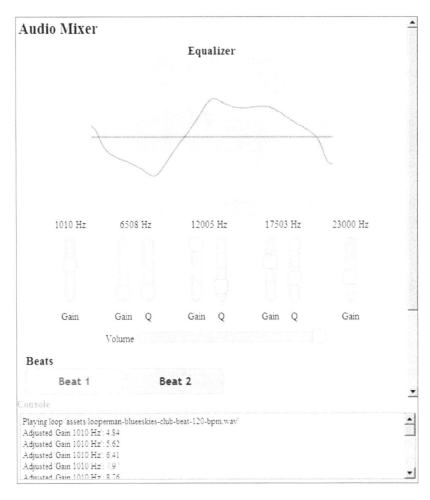

Getting ready

This time, we're building our recipe from an audio mixer template so that we can focus specifically on the equalizer implementation (you'll find the template source code in the code bundle at `tools/AudioMixerTemplate`). I recommend familiarizing yourself with its implementation—the implementation uses the Web Audio techniques and features we've covered so far.

The complete source code for this recipe is available in the code bundle at `recipes/Recipe6_1`.

How to do it...

1. Start with a clean copy of the audio mixer template. The template bundle is located at `tools/AudioMixerTemplate` in the code bundle.

2. Open `index.html` in a text editor.

3. We'll add our equalizer controls to the HTML section:

```html
<div id="appwindow">
<h2>Audio Mixer</h2>
<form>
    <div class="audiopanel" style="text-align: center;">
        <h3>Equalizer</h3>
        <canvas id="eqcanvas" width="400" height="250">
        </canvas><br>
        <div style="display: inline-block; margin: 0 20px;">
            <span id="eq_label_0"></span><br>
            <div style="display: inline-block;">
                <span id="eq_gain_0" style="display: inline-block;
height: 100px; margin: 10px;"></span><br>
                <span>Gain</span>
            </div>
        </div>
        <div style="display: inline-block; margin: 0 20px;">
            <span id="eq_label_1"></span><br>
            <div style="display: inline-block;">
                <span id="eq_gain_1" style="display: inline-block;
height: 100px; margin: 10px;"></span><br>
                <span>Gain</span>
            </div>
```

```
                <div style="display: inline-block;">
                    <span id="eq_q_1" style="display: inline-block;
height: 100px; margin: 10px;"></span><br>
                    <span>Q</span>
                </div>
            </div>
            <div style="display: inline-block; margin: 0 20px;">
                <span id="eq_label_2"></span><br>
                <div style="display: inline-block;">
                    <span id="eq_gain_2" style="display: inline-block;
height: 100px; margin: 10px;"></span><br>
                    <span>Gain</span>
                </div>
                <div style="display: inline-block;">
                    <span id="eq_q_2" style="display: inline-block;
height: 100px; margin: 10px;"></span><br>
                    <span>Q</span>
                </div>
            </div>
            <div style="display: inline-block; margin: 0 20px;">
                <span id="eq_label_3"></span><br>
                <div style="display: inline-block;">
                    <span id="eq_gain_3" style="display: inline-block;
height: 100px; margin: 10px;"></span><br>
                    <span>Gain</span>
                </div>
                <div style="display: inline-block;">
                    <span id="eq_q_3" style="display: inline-block;
height: 100px; margin: 10px;"></span><br>
                    <span>Q</span>
                </div>
            </div>
            <div style="display: inline-block; margin: 0 20px;">
                <span id="eq_label_4"></span><br>
                <div style="display: inline-block;">
                    <span id="eq_gain_4" style="display: inline-block;
height: 100px; margin: 10px;"></span><br>
                    <span>Gain</span>
                </div>
            </div>
        </div>

    ...

</form>
</div>
```

4. We'll add the equalizer functionality to `AudioLayer`. In its class constructor, we integrate the equalizer node instances into the audio layer node graph:

```
function AudioLayer( audioContext ) {
    this.audioContext = audioContext;

    // Create the volume GainNode
    this.volNode = audioContext.createGain();

    // Expose the gain control
    this.gain = this.volNode.gain;

    // Calculate the frequency metrics
    var EQ_FREQ_MARGIN = 1000;   // margin for equalizer range
    var NODES_NUM = 5;           // number of equalizer nodes

    var tempFilter = audioContext.createBiquadFilter();
    var freqMin = tempFilter.frequency.minValue
                  + EQ_FREQ_MARGIN;
    var freqMax = tempFilter.frequency.maxValue
                  - EQ_FREQ_MARGIN;
    var freqStep = (freqMax - freqMin) / (NODES_NUM - 1);

    // Create the equalizer nodes to cover the
    // frequency spectrum evenly
    var headNode = audioContext.destination;
    this.eqNodes = [];
    this.eqParms = [];
    for( var nodeIndex = 0;
         nodeIndex < NODES_NUM;
         nodeIndex++ ) {
        // Set up the filter
        var eqNode = audioContext.createBiquadFilter();

        eqNode.frequency.value =
                Math.round(freqMin + (nodeIndex * freqStep));

        if( nodeIndex == 0 ) {
            // Use a low shelf filter for the lowest filter
            eqNode.type = "lowshelf";
        } else if( nodeIndex == NODES_NUM - 1 ) {
            // Use a high shelf filter for the lowest filter
            eqNode.type = "highshelf";
```

```
        } else {
            eqNode.type = "peaking";
        }

        // Connect to the previous node
        eqNode.connect( headNode );

        // Keep track of the node
        this.eqNodes.push( eqNode );

        // Add the tweakable audio parameters to the
        // equalizer parameter array
        this.eqParms.push({
            frequency:  eqNode.frequency,
            Q:          eqNode.Q,
            gain:       eqNode.gain
        } );

        // Keep track of the head node
        headNode = eqNode;
    }

    // Connect the volume control to the last head node
    this.volNode.connect( headNode );
}
```

5. We'll add the function `AudioLayer.getEqResponse()` to return the equalizer's frequency response graph:

```
AudioLayer.prototype.getEqResponse = function( freqs ) {
    var magCombined = new Float32Array( freqs.length );

    // Get the frequency response from all the eq nodes
    var eqNodes = this.eqNodes;
    var magCurr = new Float32Array( freqs.length );
    var phaseCurr = new Float32Array( freqs.length );
    for(var eqIndex=0; eqIndex<eqNodes.length; eqIndex++ ) {
        eqNodes[ eqIndex ].getFrequencyResponse(
                freqs,
                magCurr,
                phaseCurr );

        // Combine the node magnitudes
        for( var freqIndex = 0;
```

```
                    freqIndex < freqs.length;
                    freqIndex++ ) {
                var magDb = Math.log(magCurr[ freqIndex ]) * 20;
                magCombined[ freqIndex ] += magDb;
            }
        }

        return magCombined;
    };
```

6. In `WebAudioApp`, we add the member function `updateEqGraphic()` for rendering the equalizer's response graph:

```
WebAudioApp.prototype.updateEqGraphic = function() {
    var FREQ_MIN  = 10;              // Hz
    var FREQ_MAX  = Math.round(
            this.audioContext.sampleRate * 0.5 );

    var MAG_MIN = -80;
    var MAG_MAX = 80;

    // Build the frequency response sampler list
    if( this.eqFreqs == null ) {
        var FREQS_NUM = 100;
        var FREQ_STEP = (FREQ_MAX - FREQ_MIN)
                            / (FREQS_NUM - 1);

        this.eqFreqs = new Float32Array( FREQS_NUM );
        for( var freqIndex = 0;
                freqIndex < FREQS_NUM;
                freqIndex++ ) {
            this.eqFreqs[freqIndex] = Math.round(
                FREQ_MIN + (freqIndex * FREQ_STEP) );
        }
    }

    // If we have an update scheduled, don't do anything
    if( this.eqUpdateHandle != null )
        return;

    // Schedule the graphic update
    this.eqUpdateHandle = later( 0, function(){
        this.eqUpdateHandle = null;
```

```
var canvasCtx    = $("#eqcanvas")[0]
                   .getContext( "2d" );
var canvasWidth  = canvasCtx.canvas.width;
var canvasHeight = canvasCtx.canvas.height;

// Calculate the draw steps
var stepX = canvasWidth / (FREQ_MAX - FREQ_MIN);
var stepY = canvasHeight / (MAG_MAX - MAG_MIN );

// Clear the canvas
canvasCtx.fillStyle = "#f0f0f0";
canvasCtx.fillRect( 0, 0, canvasWidth, canvasHeight );

// Draw the frequency response
var eqFreqs = this.eqFreqs;
var eqMag   = this.musicLayer.getEqResponse(eqFreqs);
var firstPt = true;
canvasCtx.beginPath();
for(var index = 0; index < eqFreqs.length; index++ ) {
    var x = Math.round(
                (eqFreqs[index] - FREQ_MIN) * stepX );
    var y = canvasHeight - Math.round(
                (eqMag[index] - MAG_MIN) * stepY );

    if( firstPt ) {
        firstPt = false;
        canvasCtx.moveTo( x, y );
    } else {
        canvasCtx.lineTo( x, y );
    }
}

canvasCtx.strokeStyle = "#ff0000";  // red line
canvasCtx.stroke();

// Draw the neutral response line
var neutralY = canvasHeight -
        Math.round( (0 - MAG_MIN) * stepY );

canvasCtx.beginPath();
canvasCtx.moveTo( 0, neutralY );
canvasCtx.lineTo( canvasWidth, neutralY );

canvasCtx.strokeStyle = "#3030ff";  // blue line
canvasCtx.stroke();
}, this );
};
```

7. Finally, we link the equalizer's HTML control widgets to its corresponding equalizer node and set up the equalizer response graph rendering in `WebAudioApp.start()`:

```
WebAudioApp.prototype.start = function() {

        ..

    // Initialize the volume slider
    this.initSlider(
            "#musicvol",
            this.musicLayer.gain,
            0.01,
            "music volume" );

    // Initialize the equalizer sliders
    var eqParms = this.musicLayer.eqParms;
    for( var nodeIndex = 0;
         nodeIndex < eqParms.length;
         nodeIndex++ ) {

        var parms = eqParms[ nodeIndex ];
        var freqValue = String( parms.frequency.value );
        this.initSlider(
            "#eq_gain_" + nodeIndex,
            parms.gain,
            0.01,
            "Gain " + freqValue + " Hz",
            {
                orientation: "vertical"
            } );
        this.initSlider(
            "#eq_q_" + nodeIndex,
            parms.Q,
            0.01,
            "Q " + freqValue + " Hz",
            {
                orientation: "vertical",
                min: 0.25,
                max: 2.5
            } );

        // Set up the label
```

```
        $("#eq_label_" + nodeIndex).text( freqValue + " Hz" );
   }

   // Set up equalizer graphics update on slider change
   var me = this;
   $( "[id^=eq_]" ).on( "slide", function() {
       me.updateEqGraphic();
   } );

   // Refresh the equalizer graphics
   this.updateEqGraphic();
};
```

Launch the application test URL in a web browser (`http://localhost/myaudiomixer`) to see the end result. Have fun playing with the mixer!

How it works...

Web Audio offers a variety of built-in audio processing nodes which can be combined to build sophisticated audio effects. One of these audio processor node types is `BiquadFilterNode`.

`BiquadFilterNode` is actually a collection of common low order filters. These low order filters form the building blocks for tonal control and more advanced filters. The following is its class definition:

1. The `type` attribute indicates the filter type represented by the instance as shown in the following code. Filter types support low-pass, high-pass, low-shelf, high-shelf, and notch filters. We'll discuss this in detail later:

   ```
   interface BiquadFilterNode : AudioNode {

       var type:String;
   ```

2. The `frequency`, `detune`, `Q`, and `gain` audio parameters affect how the filter processes its input signal. The units for `frequency`, `detune`, and `gain` are **Hz**, **cents** (1/100th of a semitone), and **dB** (decibels—a logarithmic scale for measuring gain), respectively. The units for `Q` vary depending on the type of filter. In fact, the audio parameters are interpreted differently depending on the type of filter:

   ```
   var frequency:AudioParam;      // in Hz
   var detune:AudioParam;         // in Cents
   var Q:AudioParam;              // Quality factor
   var gain:AudioParam            // in dB
   ```

The filter's applied frequency is the combined result of the `frequency` and `detune` audio parameters.

3. The `getFrequencyResponse()` method returns the frequency response for a list of frequencies as shown in the following code. Applications specify the list of frequencies (in Hz) to sample through the `frequency` parameter. The function then returns the magnitude and phase values associated with the frequencies through the array parameters `magResponse` and `phaseResponse`. Therefore, it is important that the `frequency`, `magResponse`, and `phaseResponse` arrays are of the same size:

```
function getFrequencyResponse(
            frequency:Float32Array,         // in
            magResponse:Float32Array,       // out
            phaseResponse:Float32Array );   // out
};
```

The magnitude values are returned as a gain multiplier while the phase values are returned in radians.

Make sure that the `getFrequencyResponse()` parameters are the `Float32Array` objects instead of `Array` objects! When the function parameters are not the `Float32Array` objects, the function seems to operate normally, except that the method will exit without filling `magResponse` and `phaseResponse` with the desired information.

The following table summarizes the `BiquadFilterNode` filters and how their audio parameters are interpreted:

Description	type	Interpretation		
		Frequency	gain	Q
Low-pass filter	lowpass	The cutoff frequency	Unused	The frequency drop-off steepness at the cutoff frequency
High-pass filter	highpass	The cutoff frequency	Unused	The frequency drop-off steepness at the cutoff frequency
Band-pass filter	bandpass	Center of the frequency band	Unused	The width of the frequency band

Description	type	Interpretation		
		Frequency	gain	Q
Notch filter	notch	Center of the frequency band	Unused	The width of the frequency band
Low-shelf filter	lowshelf	The upper limit of the frequencies boosted/attenuated	The boost or attenuation level	Unused
High-shelf filter	highshelf	The lower limit of the frequencies boosted/attenuated	The boost or attenuation level	Unused
Peaking filter	peaking	Center of the frequency band which is boosted/attenuated	The boost or attenuation level	The width of the frequency band
All-pass filter	allpass	Center frequency where the phase transition occurs	Unused	The transition steepness

The following is the graphical representation of the filter types:

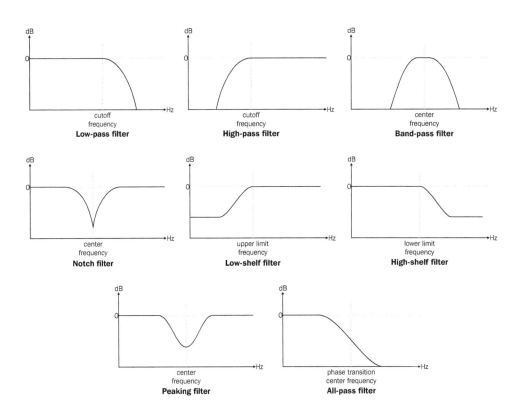

In our recipe, we build a 5-band equalizer by:

1. Inserting five `BiquadFilterNode` instances into the node graph—one for each equalizer band. These instances must be inserted in a series so that the output signal is a product of all the `BiquadFilterNode` instances.

2. Exposing each `BiquadFilterNode` instance's `gain` and `Q` audio parameters so that users can tune the equalizer behavior.

The following is the resulting node graph:

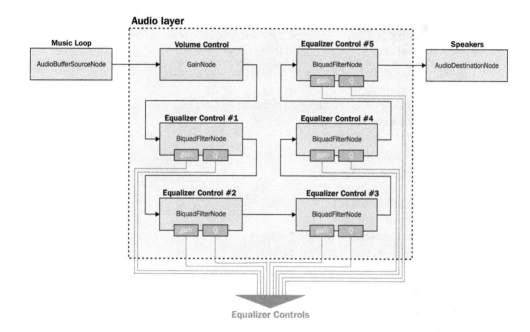

Let's take a look at the equalizer set up code in the `AudioLayer` class constructor:

1. First, we'll need to determine the default frequencies for all the equalizer bands. In order to determine this, we'll need to know the supported frequency range. We create a temporary `BiquadFilterNode` instance and sample its `frequency` audio parameter to get the frequency range. This range is reduced by `EQ_FREQ_MARGIN` at both ends yielding the cutoff frequencies for the lowest and highest equalizer bands, `freqMin` and `freqMax`. It's important that the equalizer frequency range has margins on both ends to ensure that the band filters at the ends have enough frequency range to operate properly. Finally, we calculate the default frequency step size between bands and store it in `freqStep`:

```
function AudioLayer( audioContext ) {

    . . .
```

```
// Calculate the frequency metrics
var EQ_FREQ_MARGIN = 1000;   // margin for equalizer range
var NODES_NUM = 5;           // number of equalizer nodes

var tempFilter = audioContext.createBiquadFilter();
var freqMin = tempFilter.frequency.minValue
              + EQ_FREQ_MARGIN;
var freqMax = tempFilter.frequency.maxValue
              - EQ_FREQ_MARGIN;
var freqStep = (freqMax - freqMin) / (NODES_NUM - 1);
```

2. We instantiate `BiquadFilterNode` for each equalizer band and set its `frequency` audio parameter to its default band frequency:

```
// Create the equalizer nodes to cover the
// frequency spectrum evenly
var headNode = audioContext.destination;
this.eqNodes = [];
this.eqParms = [];

for( var nodeIndex = 0;
    nodeIndex < NODES_NUM;
    nodeIndex++ ) {
    // Set up the filter
    var eqNode = audioContext.createBiquadFilter();
    eqNode.frequency.value =
        Math.round( freqMin + (nodeIndex * freqStep) );
```

3. We use a combination of peaking filters, low-shelf filters, and high-shelf filters to model the equalizer's frequency response as shown in the following code. We use a low-shelf filter and a high-shelf filter for the lowest frequency and the highest frequency equalization bands, respectively. We use peaking filters for all the other bands:

```
if( nodeIndex == 0 ) {
    // Use a low shelf filter for the lowest filter
    eqNode.type = "lowshelf";
} else if( nodeIndex == NODES_NUM - 1 ) {
    // Use a high shelf filter for the lowest filter
    eqNode.type = "highshelf";
} else {
    eqNode.type = "peaking";
}
```

Low-shelf/high-shelf versus peaking filters

It's good practice to use low-shelf/high-shelf filters over peaking filters when dealing with filtering at the frequency extremes. In theory, peaking filters should behave like low-shelf/high-shelf filters when used at the frequency extremes. In practice, the peaking filter frequency response deteriorates rapidly as it approaches the extremes. On the other hand, the low-shelf/high-shelf frequency response remains consistent.

4. We connect the `BiquadFilterNode` instances in a series to the audio context's `AudioDestinationNode` instance. Then, we cache each instance's `frequency`, `Q`, and `gain` audio parameters in `AudioLayer.eqParms` so that the applications can access the equalizer controllers directly:

```
// Connect to the previous node
eqNode.connect( headNode );

// Keep track of the node
this.eqNodes.push( eqNode );

// Add the tweakable audio parameters to the
// equalizer parameter array
this.eqParms.push({
    frequency:   eqNode.frequency,
    Q:           eqNode.Q,
    gain:        eqNode.gain
} );

// Keep track of the head node
headNode = eqNode;
```

5. Finally, we connect the layer's volume control, `AudioLayer.volNode`, to the `BiquadFilterNode` chain. The volume control is treated as the audio layer's "terminal" `AudioNode` instance—all source `AudioNode` instances must be connected to the volume control node in order to be considered as a part of the `AudioLayer` instance's node graph:

```
}

// Connect the volume control to the last head node
this.volNode.connect( headNode );
}
```

`AudioLayer.getEqResponse()` implements the logic for calculating the equalizer's frequency response:

1. Using `biquadFilterNode.getFreqResponse()`, we retrieve each equalizer band's frequency response for the target frequency list, `freqs`. The method fills `magCurr` with the response magnitude information:

```
AudioLayer.prototype.getEqResponse = function( freqs ) {
    var magCombined = new Float32Array( freqs.length );

    // Get the frequency response from all the eq nodes
    var eqNodes = this.eqNodes;
    var magCurr = new Float32Array( freqs.length );
    var phaseCurr = new Float32Array( freqs.length );
    for( var eqIndex = 0;
         eqIndex < eqNodes.length;
         eqIndex++ ) {

        eqNodes[ eqIndex ].getFrequencyResponse(
                freqs,
                magCurr,
                phaseCurr );
```

2. We convert each magnitude value from its original gain multiplier value to its dB equivalent:

```
        // Combine the node magnitudes
        for( var freqIndex = 0;
             freqIndex < freqs.length;
             freqIndex++ ) {
            var magDb = Math.log(magCurr[ freqIndex ]) * 20;
```

The formula for converting a gain multiplier to dB is as follows:

$$dB = 20 \log_{10}(gain)$$

3. Then, we sum the magnitude on a per frequency basis. The accumulated magnitude is cached in `magCombined`:

```
        magCombined[ freqIndex ] += maqDb;
```

An alternate method for calculating the combined frequency response is to multiply the gain multiplier for each sample frequency together, and then convert the combined gain multiplier into dB.

4. We return `magCombined` once all the `biquadFilterNode` frequency responses have been summed:

```
        }
    }

    return magCombined;
};
```

Finally, `WebAudioApp.updateEqGraphic()` renders the equalizer frequency response to an HTML canvas:

1. `FREQ_MIN` and `FREQ_MAX` specify the graph's rendered frequency range as shown in the following code. `FREQ_MAX` is set to the highest supported frequency so that we get a complete frequency response graph. The highest sample frequency that is supported by an `AudioContext` instance is its **Nyquist frequency**:

```
WebAudioApp.prototype.updateEqGraphic = function() {
    var FREQ_MIN  = 10;              // Hz
    var FREQ_MAX  = Math.round(
            this.audioContext.sampleRate * 0.5 );
```

 The Nyquist frequency is calculated by dividing the audio context's sample rate in half.

2. The graph renders the frequency response in dB units between the range of `MAG_MIN` and `MAG_MAX`:

```
    var MAG_MIN = -80;
    var MAG_MAX = 80;
```

3. The first time we try to render the response graph, we generate the sample frequency list and store it in `WebAudioApp.eqFreqs` as a `Float32Array` object:

```
    // Build the frequency response sampler list
    if( this.eqFreqs == null ) {
        var FREQS_NUM = 100;
        var FREQ_STEP = (FREQ_MAX - FREQ_MIN) / (FREQS_NUM - 1);

        this.eqFreqs = new Float32Array( FREQS_NUM );
        for( var freqIndex = 0; freqIndex < FREQS_NUM; freqIndex++
)
            this.eqFreqs[freqIndex] = Math.round(
                FREQ_MIN + (freqIndex * FREQ_STEP) );
    }
```

4. Because the frequency response retrieval and rendering is a fairly expensive operation, we limit the operation to occur once per update. We enforce this limit by queuing the render operation for the next update and monitoring `WebAudioApp.eqUpdateHandle` to determine when the operation has executed:

```
// If we have an update scheduled, don't do anything
if( this.eqUpdateHandle != null )
    return;

// Schedule the graphic update
this.eqUpdateHandle = later( 0, function(){
    this.eqUpdateHandle = null;
```

5. We start the frequency response graph rendering by clearing the canvas:

```
var canvasCtx = $("#eqcanvas")[0].getContext( "2d" );
var canvasWidth  = canvasCtx.canvas.width;
var canvasHeight = canvasCtx.canvas.height;

// Calculate the draw steps
var stepX = canvasWidth / (FREQ_MAX - FREQ_MIN);
var stepY = canvasHeight / (MAG_MAX - MAG_MIN );

// Clear the canvas
canvasCtx.fillStyle = "#f0f0f0";
canvasCtx.fillRect( 0, 0, canvasWidth, canvasHeight );
```

6. We retrieve the equalizer's frequency response by calling `AudioLayer.getEqResponse()` with the sample frequency list cached in `WebAudioApp.eqFreqs`:

```
// Draw the frequency response
var eqFreqs = this.eqFreqs;
var eqMag = this.musicLayer.getEqResponse( eqFreqs );
```

7. We render the response graph as a red line strip:

```
var firstPt = true;
canvasCtx.beginPath();
for(var index = 0; index < eqFreqs.length; index++) {
    var x = Math.round(
```

```
                    (eqFreqs[index] - FREQ_MIN) * stepX );
            var y = canvasHeight - Math.round(
                    (eqMag[index] - MAG_MIN) * stepY );
            if( firstPt ) {
                firstPt = false;
                canvasCtx.moveTo( x, y );
            } else {
                canvasCtx.lineTo( x, y );
            }
        }

        canvasCtx.strokeStyle = "#ff0000";  // red line
        canvasCtx.stroke();
```

8. Finally, we overlay a blue line indicating the 0 dB position.

```
        // Draw the neutral response line
        var neutralY = canvasHeight -
                Math.round( (0 - MAG_MIN) * stepY );

        canvasCtx.beginPath();
        canvasCtx.moveTo( 0, neutralY );
        canvasCtx.lineTo( canvasWidth, neutralY );

        canvasCtx.strokeStyle = "#3030ff";  // blue line
        canvasCtx.stroke();
    }, this );
};
```

There's more...

Finally we talk about the two most popularly used audio processors in Web Audio.

Other built-in Web Audio audio processors

The `biquadFilterNode` and `GainNode` instances are just two of the many built-in audio processing nodes available in Web Audio (volume manipulation is considered a form of audio processing).

The following table highlights some of the more popular audio processor classes:

Class	Description
PannerNode	Spatializes an incoming audio signal in 3D space.
DynamicsCompressorNode	Compresses the volume range of an incoming audio signal. It accomplishes this by lowering the volume of loud segments and raising the volume of soft segments.
DelayNode	Delays the incoming audio signal by a specified time delay.
ConvolverNode	Mixes an incoming audio signal with an impulse response waveform. This audio processor is a fundamental building block for reverberation effects.

The following node graph illustrates a reverberation effect constructed using Web Audio's built-in audio processing nodes:

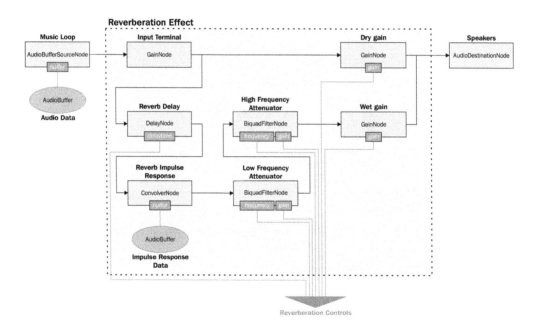

The example exposes the most common reverberation control parameters, which are:

- ▸ Reverberation delay
- ▸ Impulse response
- ▸ Reverberation high cut-off frequency
- ▸ Reverberation low cut-off frequency
- ▸ Dry/wet mix

Unfortunately, a technical implementation of the reverberation audio processor is beyond the scope of this book. Hopefully, the example will serve as an inspiration and jump point to greater and more exciting real-time audio processors on the Web.

This concludes our exploration of the Web Audio API.

Thank you for buying
Instant Audio Processing with Web Audio

About Packt Publishing

Packt, pronounced 'packed', published its first book "*Mastering phpMyAdmin for Effective MySQL Management*" in April 2004 and subsequently continued to specialize in publishing highly focused books on specific technologies and solutions.

Our books and publications share the experiences of your fellow IT professionals in adapting and customizing today's systems, applications, and frameworks. Our solution based books give you the knowledge and power to customize the software and technologies you're using to get the job done. Packt books are more specific and less general than the IT books you have seen in the past. Our unique business model allows us to bring you more focused information, giving you more of what you need to know, and less of what you don't.

Packt is a modern, yet unique publishing company, which focuses on producing quality, cutting-edge books for communities of developers, administrators, and newbies alike. For more information, please visit our website: www.packtpub.com.

Writing for Packt

We welcome all inquiries from people who are interested in authoring. Book proposals should be sent to author@packtpub.com. If your book idea is still at an early stage and you would like to discuss it first before writing a formal book proposal, contact us; one of our commissioning editors will get in touch with you.

We're not just looking for published authors; if you have strong technical skills but no writing experience, our experienced editors can help you develop a writing career, or simply get some additional reward for your expertise.

Instant HTML5 Video How-To

ISBN: 978-1-84969-364-6   Paperback: 84 pages

Over 20 practical, hands-on recipes to encode and display videos in the HTML5 video standard

1. Learn something new in an Instant! A short, fast, focused guide delivering immediate results.

2. Encode and embed videos into web pages using the HTML5 video standard

3. Publish videos to popular sites, such as YouTube or VideoBin

Instant HTML5 Local Storage How-to

ISBN: 978-1-84969-931-0   Paperback: 80 pages

Over 15 recipes to take advantage of the HTML5 Local Storage standard

1. Learn something new in an Instant! A short, fast, focused guide delivering immediate results.

2. Learn the basics of how to use the LocalStorage standard, and view the results in your browser

3. Learn how to detect when you can use LocalStorage, or when to fall back to using cookies, as well as how to convert an existing site to use LocalStorage

Please check **www.PacktPub.com** for information on our titles

Instant HTML5 Responsive Table Design How-to

ISBN: 978-1-84969-726-2   Paperback: 58 pages

Present your data everywhere on any device using responsive design techniques

1. Learn something new in an Instant! A short, fast, focused guide delivering immediate results.

2. Optimize and visualize your data using responsive design techniques

3. Understand how responsive design works and which elements you should use to make your tables responsive

Instant HTML5 Presentations How-to

ISBN: 978-1-78216-478-4   Paperback: 64 pages

Create beautiful and functional presentations using the reveal.js library, HTML5, and CSS3

1. Learn something new in an Instant! A short, fast, focused guide delivering immediate results.

2. Create presentations using HTML5 and run them straight from your browser

3. Easily publish presentations on your website by using modern web technologies

Please check **www.PacktPub.com** for information on our titles

www.ingramcontent.com/pod-product-compliance
Lightning Source LLC
Chambersburg PA
CBHW060205060326
40690CB00018B/4254